Give great presentations

How to speak confidently and make your point

BLOOMSBURY

A BLOOMSBURY REFERENCE BOOK
Created from the Bloomsbury Business Database
www.ultimatebusinessresource.com

© Bloomsbury Publishing Plc 2005

First published in 2005 by
Bloomsbury Publishing Plc
38 Soho Square
London W1D 3HB

British Library Cataloguing in Publication Data
A CIP record for this book is available from the British Library.

ISBN 0–7475–7735–8

Design by Fiona Pike, Pike Design, Winchester
Typeset by RefineCatch Limited, Bungay, Suffolk
Printed by Italy by Legoprint

All papers used by Bloomsbury Publishing are natural, recyclable products made from wood grown in well-managed forests. The manufacturing processes conform to the environmental regulations of the country of origin.

Contents

How good are your presentation skills?   iv

1 Preparing great presentations   1

2 Delivering great presentations   15

3 Fighting back against nerves   26

4 Boosting your message with your body language   35

5 Creating virtual or online presentations   47

6 Using slides and visuals in your presentation   60

7 Surviving worst-case scenarios   73

Where to find more help   88

Index   89

How good are your presentation skills?

If you're reading this as a presentation is looming, take heart! This book will help you conquer your nerves, get your message across, and give a great performance. Start here by answering these questions and reading the guidance points.

How do you feel about public speaking?
a) I hate it.
b) I prepare very carefully to avoid nerves.
c) I always enjoy it and never get too stressed.

How do you deal with nerves?
a) I don't really. I just have to get on with it.
b) I try to take it in my stride. I think being a bit nervous helps me to perform.
c) Although I do get nervous, I always pretend that I don't and bluster my way through by playing a role.

Do you practise?
a) Yes. I often try to improve my presentation at the last minute.
b) I rehearse four or five times but when I feel I have got it right, I don't tinker with it.
c) I don't bother to rehearse. I know I'll be fine.

How long do you usually make your presentations?
a) I keep it as short as possible.
b) As long as it takes to cover all the necessary ground.
c) As long as it takes—I really enjoy public speaking.

How do you deliver your presentation?
a) I often fiddle with my hair or props as I get so nervous.
b) I stand up straight and make sure I address my audience directly throughout the presentation.
c) I tend to sit down and relax.

Do you cater your presentation to your audience?
a) No, not really—I just want to get my point across.
b) Yes. I try to find out as much about them as I can beforehand.
c) Yes. I tend to aim it at the most senior people.

How long do you arrive before you are due to give a presentation?
a) I'm always a few hours early.
b) I like to leave enough time to check my equipment.
c) I'm often late.

What would you do if everything went wrong?
a) If I'm honest, I'd completely panic.
b) I'd keep smiling and try to keep calm.
c) I don't think I'd be too bothered. I'm not likely to see the audience again.

a = 1, b = 2, c = 3.
Now add up your scores.

- **8–13**: The very thought of presenting makes you nervous, so take some action to calm your nerves. Chapter **3** will help with this particularly, but chapters **1** and **2** feature lots of practical tips on planning and research that will help make your life easier too. They'll help you work out your objectives, so that you know exactly what message you want to get across. Read chapter **7** and find out that you can survive if things don't quite go to plan!

- **14–19**: Well done—you've realised that practising is the key to a great presentation! Chapter **4** will show you how you can take your performance up a notch further still by boosting what you say with the *way* you say it. Chapters **5** and **6** offer lots of advice on how you can boost your message with the clever use of visuals and images; chapter **5** is particularly useful if you're having to present 'virtually'.

- **20–23**: It's great that you enjoy presenting; it's a really useful skill to have and will stand you in good stead as you move up the career ladder. Try not to be over-confident, though, and take the time to tailor what you say to your audience—you'll really grab their attention then. Chapters **1** and **2** are particularly helpful here.

Preparing great presentations

Giving a presentation can strike fear into the heart of even the most experienced business people. It takes some courage to stand up in front of an audience and deliver a well-structured and interesting talk, and most of us at one time or another have experienced the panic, sweaty palms, blank minds, and wobbling voices that sometimes accompany this.

Being able to cope with presentations is a very valuable skill, though, whatever your job. Presentations are useful in many situations, such as pitching for business, putting a case for funding, addressing staff meetings, or even as part of the application procedure for a new job. Few people like speaking formally to an audience, but there are many real benefits and as you gain experience in giving presentations, you'll probably find that it becomes less of a worry, and even enjoyable.

This chapter offers you help on the first step of your journey towards a great presentation: preparation. It will give you some suggestions for preparing the content of what you're going to say, looking at your objectives, gearing it to your audience, and getting your points across well.

Step one: Work out your objectives

Clear objectives are the starting point for all great presentations. Start by working out your objectives—ask yourself why you're giving the talk and what you want your audience to get out of it. Think about whether using speech alone is the best way of communicating your message, or if your message might benefit from using visual aids and slides to further illustrate its main points.

When you're planning and giving the presentation, keep these objectives in mind at all times—they'll focus your thoughts. Having an objective for giving the presentation will ensure that you're not wasting anyone's time, either your audience's or your own.

For example, let's say that you're presenting a new product to your company's sales reps at your annual sales conference. Your objectives in this case may be to:

✔ introduce your product to them positively and enthusiastically

✔ talk them through the benefits of your product

✔ point out the many advantages it has over any competition

✔ explain why the target audience would want to buy it

TOP TIP

It's very important that *you* believe in what
you're going to be talking about. This is
particularly the case if you have to deliver a
difficult message, such as one related to
change or what others are likely to perceive
as bad news. These situations are bound
to be uncomfortable, and if you don't
wholeheartedly believe in your message,
others will be able to pick this up. It won't
necessarily be as a result of anything you say,
though; your body language may give it away
without you even noticing. See the next
chapter for more information on this.

Step two: Find out what you need to know about your audience

Before you plan your presentation, try as best you can to find out who is going to be in your audience, and their expectations. For example, the tone and content of a presentation to the managing director of another firm will be very different to one addressed to potential users of a product, or to one directed at people you know well. It's important that you know the extent of the audience's knowledge about the topic you'll be discussing, as their familiarity with the subject will determine the level at which you pitch the talk and the language you use (see below).

✔ Whatever the interests of your audience, try to appeal to what will motivate and interest these people. For example, if you're talking to senior people in your company about a new product, you might want to include information about how it can be produced cost-effectively; if you're talking about a new way of doing things, stress how much more effective it will make your team. If you're talking to reps who'll be selling the product for you, you need to highlight how much better it is than the competition. As you can see from these examples, you need to 'tune in' as far as you can to your audience's needs. A few hours doing the groundwork is time very well spent.

Step three: Make sure you've got your facts straight

Once you know why you're speaking and who you're talking to, you can firm up your ideas about what you're going to say.

Get back to basics by checking that you have all the main facts straight. For example, if you're talking about a product or service, make sure you know:

■ its current name (remember that this may have changed many times!)

- its price
- when it will be ready
- what it's meant to do
- how it works, if appropriate
- benefits
- what the competition is

If you're talking about a new process, find out about:

- why you're changing from an existing way of doing things
- what the changes are
- when they'll take effect
- what benefits they'll bring

TOP TIP

If you're giving your presentation just after you've come back from holiday or a business trip, take a few moments to check a few key facts with colleagues before you speak. Some key elements of your presentations (such as prices, names, delivery dates) may have changed while you've been away, and the last thing you need is to have someone pipe up from the back to correct you. It will boost your confidence to know that you're on top of things!

Step four: Begin writing your speech

When it comes to presentations, there's no substitute for detailed preparation and planning. While everyone prepares in different ways, all of which develop with experience, here are a few key points to bear in mind while you're preparing.

✔ Start by breaking up the task of preparing your speech into manageable units. Once you know the length of the presentation—let's say 15 minutes—break up the time into smaller units and allocate sections of your speech to each unit. For example, you might want to give two minutes to a general introduction, six minutes to a discussion of your main theme, two minutes to sum up key points, and five minutes to take questions. All of this will depend very much on your topic and audience, however, so don't try and shoe-horn your presentation into a very rigid format—keep things fluid if you need to.

✔ Note down all the points you want to make, and order them logically. This will help you develop the framework and emphasis of the presentation.

✔ Keep your presentation short and simple if you possibly can, as it will be easier for you to manage and remember. A shorter presentation is usually more effective from the audience's point of view, too, as most people dislike long presentations and will not necessarily remember any more from them.

TOP TIP

If you need to provide more detail, it's a good idea to supply a printed handout to your audience *at the end* of the presentation. This is the best time to do it, as otherwise you'll be fighting to make yourself heard against the rustling paper.

✔ Avoid overloading your talk with facts and figures; a few well-placed numbers can help illustrate a point, but it can be hard to maintain an audience's interest if they are being bombarded with figures. Instead, use some graphs or charts to illustrate what you're saying. Aim to identify two or three key points, and think about ways you can get these across creatively.

✔ Don't use too much jargon. It may be tempting, especially if you work in a technical industry, but bear your audience in mind at all times—if you've followed the steps above and done some research on them, you'll know how familiar they are with your theme, and not everyone will be a specialist. If you do need to use abbreviations or acronyms, explain early on what they mean so that everyone can follow you. You can always recap on your handout, if you provide one, or list them on your website.

Step five: Think about using visual aids and equipment

Some presentations may benefit from the use of visual aids of some type, such as acetates for an overhead projector (OHP), or a computer presentation package such as PowerPoint. Remember that visual aids should only be used as signposts during the presentation, to help the audience focus on the main point you're trying to make.

✔ If you do decide to use them, try not to cram too much information onto one slide or screen, as you'll lose your audience's attention while they try to read everything on it. Make sure the audience can see the information by using big, bold, simple lettering, and bear in mind that images are often far more effective than words.

Turn to Chapter 6 for step-by-step advice on this topic.

Step six: Practise!

OK, so you know what you want to say, who you're aiming it at, and your slides are ready. It's time to put everything together and practise.

✔ Practise as much as you need to make sure that you're very familiar with your speech—allow plenty of time for rehearsal before the event. Even if the presentation has been sprung on you with very little notice, run yourself through it at least three or four times. Don't panic if your mind goes blank when you start off; keep calm, go back to the beginning, and start again. At points you may feel that you'll never get it right, but you will and you'll find a rhythm that swings you along.

TOP TIP

Once you're confident that your presentation is right, don't tinker with it! *You* may have heard it many times, but your audience won't have. Changing things at the last minute is just giving you more stress that you don't need.

✔ Also practise your speech using the equipment you intend to use; slide projectors and video machines should be tested in advance to make sure you know how to operate them, and your laptop or PC should be checked out to make sure that it hasn't developed some dreadful problem.

✔ Have a contingency plan to cope with any unforeseen mishaps. For example, you might want to print out copies of your slides so that if the computer breaks down and there's an OHP to hand, you can show them that way. If the worst comes to the worst, you can distribute them as handouts at the end of your talk. See Chapter 7 for more help on what to do if things don't go to plan.

TOP TIP

If you've saved your talk onto a CD-ROM that you're going to run from a computer on-site, it's a good idea to also e-mail the file to an e-mail account that you can get into wherever you're giving the presentation. This could be your work e-mail address if it allows remote access, or an Internet-based e-mail provider such as Hotmail, AOL, or Yahoo. This means that if the CD-ROM goes haywire for any reason, you can download the presentation from your e-mail to the computer you're using, and carry on as normal.

✔ Time your speech during rehearsals to make sure that your speech is taking the time you'd estimated. Remember that you'll probably need to allow time at the end for a question-and-answer session. Don't bring all your notes into the presentation, but instead list the main points on numbered cards, known as cue cards, to provide reminders.

TOP TIP

Using cards rather than pieces of paper has lots of advantages. You can move through the cards much more easily (and quietly, especially if your hands shake!) than you can do with sheaves of paper, and you can also add notes to yourself to help you speak

more confidently. This can be anything
from 'breathe!' to 'emphasis here' to
'pause here'—whatever works best for you.

Step seven: Think about the venue

✔ If you're giving your presentation on home turf, book or
arrange an appropriately-sized room as soon as you
know you're going to have to speak. Make sure there's
enough seating for your audience, and that lighting,
ventilation, and heating are all working properly.

TOP TIP

Ask a colleague to stand at the back of the
room in which you're going to speak so that
you can make sure you're speaking loudly
enough. If the room is very big (a boardroom
in a large organisation, say) or even a small
one with poor acoustics, it might be worth
finding or asking the company to invest in a
microphone. They're inexpensive (from £10
upwards) and can be used time and again.

✔ Organise some refreshments for participants such as
tea, coffee, and water. You also need to make sure there
will be no interruptions, for example by phone calls, fire
drills, or people accidentally entering the room. Put a

sign up on the door that states the time the meeting is due to begin and how long it will go on for. If your talk has a title, such as 'Motivating your sales team', or 'New products for ABC Ltd', you could add that too.

TOP TIP

If your company has a receptionist, it's a good idea to let him or her know that there'll be an influx of guests on the day. He or she can then point them in the right direction and let you know when they start to arrive so that you can be ready to greet them.

✔ Whether you're presenting at your own office or elsewhere, you must make sure that any equipment or props you need are available and set up properly before the presentation starts. If you're presenting away from your office, for example, at a conference or a client's premises, it's a good idea to visit the site beforehand to make sure it has everything you're expecting. It's even a good idea to check out where the switches or plug points are, so that you don't get caught out on the day.

Common mistakes

✗ **You don't find out about your audience**
A good knowledge of the audience is absolutely crucial in finding the correct pitch. It's no good blinding your

audience with technical jargon if they only have a basic grasp of the subject. Similarly, a very knowledgeable audience will soon switch off if you spend the first few minutes going over the basics.

✗ You talk for too long

If your presentation absolutely *has* to be longer than 20 minutes, insert some breaks so that your audience remains fresh and interested and you can have a sip of water to keep you going.

✗ You don't check the room and equipment

This can be disastrous! Imagine, for example, arriving and finding that there's no facility for delivering PowerPoint presentations, and you have no other method of showing slides. Make sure you're familiar with the environment in which you'll be presenting.

STEPS TO SUCCESS

✔ Make sure you have clear objectives for your presentation. Know what you want to say and why.

✔ Believe in what you're saying; if you're unsure of or unhappy about your message, the audience will pick up on it.

✔ Find out about your audience. This will help you 'pitch' the presentation well.

✔ Make sure you're up-to-speed about all the basic facts relevant to your presentation, such as prices, deadlines, specifications, benefits, competition, and so on.

✔ Prepare, plan, and practise thoroughly.

Useful links

Mind Tools:
**www.mindtools.com/CommSkll/
PresentationPlanningChecklist.htm**
SpeechTips.com:
www.speechtips.com/preparation.html

Delivering great presentations

A presentation is an ideal environment for you to promote your ideas, your products, or your services. You have a captive audience, are able to provide them with relevant information, and can answer any questions they may have on the spot. For a presentation to be a success you must be able to hold the attention of the audience and leave them wanting to know more.

Some people are natural presenters, while others find it more difficult. If you fall into this group, don't worry; practice and feedback from previous audiences will help you develop all the necessary skills. In Chapter 1, we found out about how to get ready for the presentation; this chapter will help you deliver it with confidence and style.

Step one: Look at the structure of your presentation

Structure is essential for any presentation. There should be an introduction, a main body, and a conclusion. You can be witty, controversial, or even outrageous if the mood of the presentation allows, but whatever approach you try, your chief aim is to arouse the audience's curiosity, and to get your message across.

I Introduce your presentation

The introduction to your presentation needs to attract your audience's interest and attention.

A good opening will also boost your own confidence, because if you start well, the rest should follow easily. Plan your opening words carefully for maximum impact: they should be short, sharp, and to the point.

✔ If appropriate (that is, if you're speaking externally at a conference or internally to people you've never met before, such as prospective customers or suppliers), introduce yourself briefly. There's no need to go into too much detail; just tell them your name, job title, and the broad subject you're talking about.

✔ Let your audience know how long your presentation will take, as this will prepare them to focus for the period of time you expect to speak.

✔ Summarise the contents of your presentation, so that your audience can work out how much information they'll need to absorb.

✔ Explain how the presentation will work in terms of the audience's interaction with you; tell them if you'll be taking questions at the end, or if you're happy for them to pipe up as you go along.

TOP TIP

Explaining the key points in the first few sentences will also help your mind to focus on the task in hand, and refresh your memory on the major points of your presentation. It sometimes helps to get started if you can learn your first few sentences by heart.

---

2 Make an impact in the main section of the presentation

It goes without saying that the main section of your presentation will be driven by the points you want to make.

✔ For maximum impact, use short, sharp, and simple language that will keep your audience's attention and also make sure that your message is being understood.

TOP TIP

Include only one idea per sentence and pause after each one, so that you make a mental 'full stop'.

✔ While you do need to be precise in what you say, make sure you don't sound too stilted or as if you're

---

reading something out of a book—it's good to give the impression of spontaneity.

✔ However nervous you feel, stick to your original plan for your presentation, and don't go off at a tangent on a particular point and miss the thread. Why not try using metaphors and images to illustrate points? This will give impact to what you say, and help your audience to remember what you've said.

3 Conclude your presentation

Close by summing up the key points of what you've covered. The closing seconds of your presentation are as crucial as the opening sentence as they give you an opportunity to really hammer home your point. To make the most of this, think about what action you'd like your audience to take after the presentation is over and then inspire them to do it.

For example, let's say you've been presenting your new star product to your company's most loyal customers. You want them to love the product as much as you do, to buy it in large numbers, and to sell it with gusto. Remember that this is where your enthusiasm for, and belief in, your message can truly make a difference, so:

✔ be brief, but speak clearly without rushing

✔ quickly restate the product's advantages or benefits

✔ emphasise your hopes for the product (for example, you believe it will be the market leader in X months' time)

✔ if it's in your gift, offer them an incentive, such as if they buy early, an X % discount or a multi-buy offer

Step two: Think about your posture and delivery

Now that you know what you'll be saying, it's time to think about how you can say it best and definitely make a splash.

✔ Maintain eye contact and address your audience directly throughout your presentation.

✔ Be aware of your stance, posture, and gestures without being too self-conscious. Don't slouch, as you'll look unprofessional. Standing up straight will make you appear more confident and will also help you to project your voice better.

TOP TIP

Always stand, rather than sit, when you're doing a presentation. Don't fiddle, for example with a pencil or a piece of paper; try to keep still and avoid moving around excessively. All these things are distracting for an audience, and will mean that they're missing important points you're trying to get across.

✔ Remember that your audience has come to learn something. Try to sound authoritative, sincere, and enthusiastic. If you don't sound as if you believe in yourself, this will come across to the audience.

✔ Think about the way in which you're speaking. Most people need to articulate their words more clearly when addressing an audience. There's usually no opportunity for the audience to ask you to repeat a word they've missed, so aim to sound the vowels and consonants of words clearly.

✔ Think about the expression in your voice too. Try to vary the volume, pitch, and speed of delivery to underline your meaning and to keep up your audience's interest.

TOP TIP

Think about your *facial* expressions too. Obviously, if you're talking about a contentious issue or have to tell a group of people bad news, you're not going to be all singing, all dancing as you take the podium, but if your presentation is a more general one, or sales-orientated, it's good to smile! Smiling at your audience will give the impression that you're at your ease and that you're looking forward to talking to them.

Step three: Answer any questions

Some people prefer to take questions at the end of a presentation rather than have their flow of concentration interrupted while they're speaking. This is a good strategy if you're nervous or if you're talking about a complicated or very technical subject—it's all too easy to lose your way.

✔ If you do take questions at the end of a talk, give your audience an idea of how much time you have to spend on it; this may be an issue if you're just one of a number of people speaking in a particular session, as if you run over, everyone will start running late.

✔ If someone asks you a question and you don't know the answer, be honest and tell the other person that you'll find out what they need to know and get back to them separately. This will save time, and also prevent you from giving an incorrect answer.

✔ Encourage interesting discussions between members of the audience by throwing general discussion points open to the floor once you've said your piece (or even if you haven't!). This tactic may be appropriate if you're speaking to an audience made up of your peers or of specialists in a certain subject; you may all learn something from it.

Step four: Make a dignified exit

Once the question and answer session is over, you're just about done. All that remains is for you to say thank you to the audience for listening. If you have handouts to circulate, now is the time to do it. It's a good idea to include your contact details on these handouts so that people can get in touch with you about questions that occur to them later, or hopefully to indicate some interest in what you've been talking about. Thank them for their feedback and keep in touch if you can; giving presentations is a great way to network and build up your contact list.

TOP TIP
Watch where you're going! If you've been nervous about doing your presentation, you're bound to be heartily relieved that it's all over. In your eagerness to take your seat elsewhere, don't rush off stage in case there are tricky steps to negotiate. Also keep an eye out for cables, leads, plugs, or even chairs in the way that you don't want to bump into and ruin the great impression you've made.

Common mistakes

✗ **You're not enthusiastic**
If *you're* not interested in what you have to say, don't expect your audience to be. Listening to a single voice

for 20 minutes or more can be difficult for an audience, so you have to inject some enthusiasm into what you're saying if you are to keep them with you (and awake!). To help keep things going, activities or discussion with your audience, as mentioned above, can help a great deal.

✗ You speak too quickly

Don't rush your presentation; it's important to take your time. It's hard not to rush, especially when you're nervous and want the whole thing over with as soon as possible, but the audience will find it difficult to understand you, or to keep up, if you talk too fast. Make sure you summarise your main points every five minutes or so, or as you reach the end of a section. This will help to pick out the most important issues for your audience, and it's then more likely that they'll remember the central issues long after you've finished your presentation. As discussed in Chapter 1, practising with a colleague or friend will help a lot here, as he or she can tell you how you're doing in terms of the speed of your delivery.

✗ You don't check the equipment

There's nothing more irritating for an audience who have all made an effort to turn up on time, than to have to sit around and wait while you struggle to get your laptop to work, or sort your slides out. Make sure everything is exactly in place well before your audience begins to arrive. A technician should be on hand if you're planning to use sophisticated technology.

✗ You don't interact with the audience

Be careful not to look at the floor during your presentation, or to direct your speech at one person. Try and draw your whole audience into the presentation by glancing at everyone's faces, in a relaxed and unhurried way, as you make your points. Keeping in tune with your audience in this way will also help you judge if people are becoming bored. If you do detect that people are glazing over, you could try to change the tempo of your presentation to refocus their attention.

✗ You're late!

We all have days when absolutely everything seems to go wrong, but as far you can, try to make turning up late to your own presentation the last thing you need to worry about. Leave yourself twice as much time for your journey than you think you'll need. This will allow for getting lost several times en route. If you're driving or taking the train, check your local news before you leave to see if there are any hold-ups. If the presentation is more than a few hours' drive away and you're on quite early, see if your company will foot the bill for you staying overnight nearby.

Useful links

BusinessTown.com:
www.businesstown.com/presentations/index.asp

iVillage.co.uk:
**www.ivillage.co.uk/workcareer/survive/prodskills/
articles/0,,156471_156690,00.html**
SpeechTips.com:
www.speechtips.com/delivering.html

Fighting back against nerves

Being overcome by nerves can be a completely debilitating experience that sabotages our ability to communicate well and to demonstrate how well we can do our job. If you're prone to feeling nervous, presentations are probably one of the most stressful situations you can be placed in. The body's nervous reaction to speaking in public, whether it's making a presentation to customers or colleagues, or even making an intervention during an internal meeting can, if left unchecked, rob us in just a few seconds of the confidence and experience built up during the course of our career.

If you *do* suffer from nerves in some work situations, take comfort in knowing that you're not alone and that with the help of a few simple techniques, you can kick nerves into touch. It's always tempting to think that a problem will just go away, but tackling nerves will offer a range of positive results, including being able to be yourself, contributing to events in the way you know you can deep down, and getting the amazing next job you deserve. Overcoming nerves is a great first step on the journey to full confidence.

Step one: Start off with some positive thinking

It's always hard to be objective when you're very worried about something, but it really is the first step on the road to taking charge of yourself. If you see yourself failing at something in your mind's eye, you're much more likely to end up with a disaster on your hands. Try to get your imagination under control and instead of seeing yourself getting it all spectacularly wrong, see yourself succeeding brilliantly. Your body will follow the cues from your mind, so train your mind to be positive and to 'invite' success for yourself.

TOP TIP
Don't let negative images or words creep in
and get in the way of your preparation; if
you feel your positive attitude starting to
slip, take a short break and start again.

Step two: Breathe!

When people get nervous, they panic and speak before they've thought things through. If you're worried that your mouth may run away with you, manage your breathing. Most people aren't particularly good at doing this, but it's the key to giving yourself space to observe and hear what's going on. This is an important technique to learn if you have to participate in meetings or if people will be asking you questions as part of your presentation—being sensitive to the needs of others and different situations is an important part of being able to say the right thing at the right time.

TOP TIP

If you're in an important meeting that you want to contribute to, give yourself time to take in the information you need and formulate what you're going to say. Don't rush in, but breathe calmly and don't worry about short silences.

Step three: Don't let shyness be a barrier

If you're naturally a shy person, then public speaking can seem a huge barrier to overcome. Strangely, though, some of the best presenters are introverts and many have severe bouts of nerves before taking the stage and delivering a polished performance.

One good way of lessening the fear of public speaking is to think of it as having a conversation, rather than giving a talk. It also helps to break the ice by meeting a few people from your audience first; this will help you make a connection with them that you can use and build on while you're on the platform. Be friendly, smile, look people in the eyes, ask questions if appropriate, and take the listening time to breathe, relax, and enjoy the experience if you can.

Step four: Understand the physical effects of worry

Although the effects of a bout of nerves show themselves physically, it's actually our state of mind that triggers them. Fears that we'll make a fool of ourselves or that we won't achieve our aims commonly drive our nervous reactions, which are often known as the 'fight or flight' response.

Thousands of years ago, when we were surviving in a physically hostile world that was populated by human predators or enemies, our fight or flight response enabled us to fuel our strength and overpower a beast or build our speed and outrun a something that was threatening us. In the moment of need, adrenalin would be released, our hearts would pump faster, our blood would be super-oxygenated, and our muscles would be fed to achieve higher levels of performance. This is what enabled human beings to survive and build the (relatively) safe, sophisticated, and cerebral world that we enjoy today. However, in spite of our successful emergence from the primitive world, our bodies still react to fear—whether it be real or imagined—in the same way.

When we're giving a presentation, our fear of failure gives rise to the fight or flight response along with its characteristic bodily reactions, but these now have nowhere to go. We don't take flight and neither do we fight, but instead stand still, tell ourselves not to be so silly, and try to combat the panic. By this stage, there's no point in trying to use our mind to control the effects of fear as our body has taken control. The fact that we can't do anything about it gives rise to further feelings of anxiety and sends a message to the body to try harder because the threat has not disappeared and there's still work to be done. More adrenalin . . . faster heart beat . . . busy muscles . . . and so it goes on. Trying to break this cycle is the challenge of overcoming nerves and it can be tackled in two ways; through the mind and through the body.

| Overcome nerves through the mind

✔ Use visualisation as a technique for removing fear. Imagine your audience receiving your information enthusiastically, being interested in what you're saying, and applauding when you've finished. Enhance this image with feelings of satisfaction, achievement, and pride. Watch yourself leave the spotlight feeling confident and happy to acknowledge people who come up to you afterwards to congratulate you on your performance.

✔ Think through your presentation or performance beforehand so that you're both practically and mentally prepared. If you're likely to be asked questions on your presentation, imagine what these might be and prepare some answers. If it helps, write them down, read over them a few times and tick them off your 'checklist' of things to prepare.

✔ Get as much information as possible. This will help you target your talk appropriately and demonstrate that you understand your audience's perspective and needs well. Being able to show that you've taken the time to do this will help win them over and put them on your side.

Working through the exercises above will help remove the perceived threat you fear and will fill your mind with positive images. Cancelling out the threat in any given situation means that you're a lot less likely to have an adverse physical response to it.

2 Overcome nerves through the body

Some of these well-known relaxation techniques will help prevent your body from triggering the 'fear response'.

✔ Spend a few minutes to calm your breathing and to take attention away from the impending performance. Breathe deeply into your stomach, hold your breath for a few seconds, and breathe out again. Do this several times in a quiet spot away from the action.

✔ Relax your body. Sit in a chair and concentrate on each muscle group one by one. Working from your feet to your forehead, contract and then relax your muscles. Feel the difference. If you find yourself becoming tense again, go back to the problem area and try again, breathing deeply and steadily as you do so.

✔ Have some water before your performance to prevent you from drying up and keep another glass beside you so that you can refresh your mouth as you go.

TOP TIP
Overcoming nerves is hard work, but it's well worth spending the time to do it. Succeeding means that you'll be able to express yourself well and with confidence in any situation and will help you in all areas of your life.

Common mistakes

✗ **You put yourself under too much pressure**
It's completely counter-productive to beat yourself up about getting nervous. What is the point? The best thing to do is to set yourself reasonable goals, take things one step at a time, and give yourself an opportunity to celebrate each small success and build upon it incrementally. If you challenge yourself by putting yourself in extreme situations, you run the risk of failing in those extremes and it can be very difficult to recover from that. Be gentle with yourself and try to build your confidence steadily and soundly.

✗ You pretend you don't suffer from nerves

When people want to appear confident and competent, they often won't own up to suffering from nerves and end up playing a part, rather than being themselves. This is a common mistake which at best makes it seem as if you're suppressing the real 'you', but at worst, can make you seem arrogant. Putting on masks can be helpful in some situations, for example, if the *real* you is hidden somewhere in the role that you've decided to act out, but removing who you are by 'being someone else' isn't a good way to overcome nerves. Hiding yourself away won't help and in fact sometimes it's just better to acknowledge your perceived short-comings and turn to someone who can help you find an appropriate way through.

✗ You think the problem will go away

Many would-be presenters who are overcome by nerves avoid dealing with them, thinking that they just have to get through their ordeal and somehow arrive at the other side. This is perfectly true, but it can be life-enhancing to face your fears and find a dignified way through. Often when we look our fears in the face, they begin to subside, especially if we practise techniques to master them. Rehearsing is extremely helpful, whether it's in front of friends, family, or even the mirror. If you're able to video yourself rehearsing, so much the better; you'll learn a lot.

Useful links

businessknowhow.com:

www.businessknowhow.com/growth/public-speaking.htm

fearofpublicspeaking.net:

www.fearofpublicspeaking.net/public_speaking_nerves.htm

Total Success:

www.tsuccess.dircon.co.uk/presentationnerves.htm

Boosting your message with your body language

We all know that real communication is not just a matter of making a noise. But did you realise just how little impact *what* we actually say has on people we're speaking to? In a face-to-face situation, like a presentation, between 55 and 65 per cent of your meaning is communicated by your body language—your posture, movements, and facial expressions—and 38 per cent comes from your tone of voice. That leaves just seven per cent to be conveyed by the words you use!

In addition, researchers also agree that the verbal part of the communication is used to convey information, while the non-verbal part is used to convey values, feelings, and attitudes—the things that build rapport.

It's obvious, then, that if you can learn to understand and control body language in a conscious way, you can make an enormous difference to the impact you have on your audience. This chapter will help you to use the different forms of non-verbal communication to help get your message across effectively and to build rapport with your listeners.

Step one: Make a good entrance

People, like animals, are territorial and instinctively perceive new spaces—like an unfamiliar presentation room—as hostile territory. As a result, it's natural, if you have not been in the room before, to decrease your speed as you enter it, and this can make you look as if you lack confidence. There are a number of things you can do about this:

- ✔ be in the room first, before your audience arrives, so that you already 'own' the space

- ✔ familiarise yourself with the room before the presentation, so that when you do enter you are more relaxed and in charge

- ✔ make a point of going into the room at an even speed, or even stopping at the door before entering

Step two: Use positive postures

One of the biggest giveaway indications of nerves is your posture. And interestingly enough if you look nervous, rather than getting people's sympathy, you tend to make your audience inclined to feel hostile towards you. Self-defence teachers know this: they teach their pupils to carry themselves in a self-confident and upright manner, as people who walk in a timid or frightened way are much more likely to be victims of attack.

To make sure that your posture doesn't betray your nerves as you speak:

✔ stand up straight with your feet slightly apart; keep your head up, and think generally about taking up as much space as you can. It might help to keep in mind the saying, 'think tall and you'll *be* tall'—this will automatically help you to adopt a much more confident posture.

✔ don't hold your arms in front of your body too much. People feeling nervous or unsure of themselves will often 'protect' themselves: in other words, they adopt a posture that protects a vulnerable area. Men might stand with their hands clasped in front of their genitals, and women tend to fold their arms across their chests. Nothing can make you look more nervous than standing in front of a presentation audience with a folder clasped to your front!

TOP TIP
If you can avoid it, don't have any piece of furniture or other object between you and your audience—it can act as a barrier and create a distance between you. However, if you find you have a tendency to shuffle your feet nervously, you could try positioning a table behind you where you can lean back on the edge of it.

Step three: Be natural with gestures

It's easy to worry too much about gestures. With a few exceptions, most gestures are fine—providing they feel natural to you. After all, for most people, gestures are an extension of their personality and it can make you feel uncomfortable and unnatural if you try to repress them.

Neil Kinnock, the former leader of the Labour Party, gave an intriguing example of someone trying to repress his natural gesturing habits during the 1992 general election campaign. His tendency to wave his arms around was interpreted by some as a sign of impetuousness, when in fact his aim was to show he could be trusted to run the country and command the respect of other world leaders, so campaign organisers advised him to grip the sides of the rostrum. Camera shots from the rear, however, show clearly how he slid his hands up and down and gripped the edges during his speeches as he tried to keep a grip on his enthusiasm. It clearly wasn't comfortable for him to have his natural exuberance restrained in that way.

Having said this, there are a few useful things to remember about gestures:

✔ never make a rude one, obviously!

✔ try not to make the same gesture too many times, or it will turn into a mannerism that will distract your audience.

They might find it tempting to count how many times you wag your forefinger, rather than listening to what you're saying.

✔ be on the look out for distracting habits you acquire only when you're under stress, such as foot shuffling or lip licking. If you know what these are, you might be able to eliminate them, or at least minimise them.

✔ if you find it difficult to know what to do with your hands, you could try using a 'prop'. Many people use props to reinforce their messages, the most common being extensions of the hand such as a pen or pointer. Using a prop extends the space taken up by your body—and hence your territory—and you are perceived as more confident and powerful.

TOP TIP

No matter how nervous you are, try to avoid hand-to-face gestures such as touching your nose or rubbing your eye. These often mean you're not entirely comfortable with your subject matter, and can signify that you're not being completely honest about something. Even if your listeners don't know this consciously, they will pick up on your discomfort.

Step four: Keep up eye contact

It's true of all human interactions to say that the more eye contact we have with someone, the closer we tend to feel to them—and they to us. Often we will avoid eye contact with someone we don't like, and if we do make it, we will adopt an unemotional stare, rather than a friendly gaze.

✔ When you're giving a presentation, keep your eye contact with people as normal as possible. Look at everyone in the room, not just person in the middle at the front who you feel is on your side. That way each member of your audience will begin to feel that they have forged some sort of personal bond with you, and will be more receptive to your message.

TOP TIP
There are two useful things to remember about eye contact. Firstly, lowered eyes make you look shy. Secondly, people will naturally follow your gaze and if you keep looking at the ceiling, so will they.

Step five: Keep an eye on your timing

In normal conversation, another element that conveys information (often unconsciously) is the speed at which you talk. Speaking slowly can sometimes indicate that you're uncertain of what you're saying; speaking quickly may show that you're anxious or excited. These rules still apply to some degree when you're making a presentation, which may make you feel as if you're stuck between a rock and a hard place. As ever, though, going for the middle ground is much the safest option.

✔ Although it's important to speak slowly enough to enable your audience to hear what you're saying, don't overdo it or you'll sound hesitant. Conversely, you also need to guard against gabbling—it's a natural tendency to speak faster than usual if you're nervous and if you're normally a fast talker anyway, you can completely lose your audience!

Step six: Watch your tone and mannerisms

The *manner* in which you speak during your presentation is almost more important than anything else. If you think about it, even a simple word like 'hello' can have multiple different meanings—friendly, hostile, surprised, suspicious, offhand, and many others—depending on how you say it, so you need to be careful about what tone of voice you use. There are a number of things to think about here.

✔ Try to sound friendly, but not so casual that you lose your authority.

✔ At the same time, don't be too bossy—this is a presentation, not a lecture.

✔ It's better to be too loud than too soft: nothing is more trying for an audience that a mumbling presenter.

✔ Ask someone you trust to listen to you and check that you are not swallowing words (easy to do when you're nervous)—in other words, that the ends of your sentences don't die away and become inaudible. To a listener, this makes it seem as if the presentation is repeatedly grinding to a halt.

✔ Bear in mind that too many 'ums', 'ers' and hesitations make you sound unprofessional and can be irritating to listen to. Plenty of rehearsal should solve this issue.

TOP TIP

As with physical gestures, most catch phrases—'as I say', 'basically', 'you know', for example—are fine unless they're used too frequently, when they become a distracting mannerism. Again, when you practise, ask someone to keep an ear out for things like this. You'll be so used to saying them, that you won't notice you're doing it!

Step seven: Remember your facial expressions

As with eye contact, people's emotions towards us are influenced by our facial expressions. In fact, this is so much the case that if someone continually shows the 'wrong' facial expressions, or doesn't change their expression at all, we find it hard to warm to them.

While this doesn't mean you should grin manically at your audience throughout your presentation, it does mean that you don't have to be too guarded in your expressions—and it won't ruin your image or make you appear unprofessional if you smile occasionally. In fact, smiling will help put you and your audience at ease. It's not appropriate at all times, of course—if you're delivering bad news of some type, for example—but in the normal run of things, it does no harm.

Step eight: Match your clothes to the occasion

According to the experts, people form 90 per cent of their opinion about someone within the first 90 seconds of meeting them, which means that your audience will be making judgments about you long before you even open your mouth.

What you wear is therefore your first means of communicating something about yourself, and will help your audience to relate to you . . . or not. As a rough rule of thumb, people tend to like people who are like them—so it's best to dress in the same sort of way as those you'll be presenting to. If you're presenting informally to a group of colleagues, for example, you can wear normal office attire, while a more formal suit might be better for a meeting of government bureaucrats.

If in doubt, it's probably best to err on the side of restraint. That way, the worst you can do is to present a blank canvas that doesn't distract your audience from what you have to say. After all, you want your *message* to be the point of focus in your presentation, not your personality.

Common mistakes

✗ You lack 'congruence'
Because body language is something that occurs naturally, whether or not we are conscious of it, it's impossible to control every last aspect of it. This means that if you are talking about something you don't really believe in, or if you're not entirely comfortable with what you are saying, your body language will subtly 'leak' this somewhere along the line. This lack of 'congruence' between your words and your body language will be picked up on by your audience, and they are likely to feel suspicious and distrustful of you and your message. The only answer is to be authentic in what you say

and your body language will reinforce that message
naturally.

✗ You over-do things

When you become conscious of all the ways in which
you communicate non-verbally with others, it can
suddenly become terribly easy to over-do them . . . your
eye contact is a little *too* intense, your posture a little *too*
confident, your gestures a little *too* controlled, and so on.
And, just as is the case with a lack of congruence, this
can make you come across as insincere and inauthentic
and may turn your audience against you. To be effective,
body language must be subtle and seem completely
natural—and the only way to achieve this is to practise
over and over again. Try watching yourself in a mirror as
you rehearse your presentation, or ask someone you
trust to observe you and give you honest feedback.
Eventually, if you practise enough, controlling your
body language will become second nature to you.

STEPS TO SUCCESS

✔ Make a positive entrance so that you, and not your
audience, 'own' the space.

✔ Adopt a confident posture that will reduce any inclination
in people to be hostile towards you.

✔ Be natural in your gestures, while taking care that no
individual gesture becomes a mannerism through being
used too frequently.

✔ Maintain regular eye contact with all members of your audience to build rapport.

✔ Speak at the right speed—not so slowly that you sound hesitant, but not so fast that you gabble.

✔ Check that your tone of voice makes your message friendly and accessible, while still retaining its authority.

✔ Don't worry about being too guarded in your facial expressions, or you may come across as odd.

✔ Dress to flatter your audience—in other words, in a similar way to them.

Useful links

Culture at Work:

www.culture-at-work.com/nvcnegotiation.html

NLP training and resources:

www.altfeld.com/mastery/seminars/desc-sb1.html

The non-verbal dictionary of gestures, signs, and body language:

http://members.aol.com/nonverbal2/diction1.htm

PPI Business NLP:

www.ppimk.com

Rider University Clinical Psychology Department:

www.rider.edu/users/suler/bodylang.html

Creating virtual or online presentations

Online or virtual presentations are rather different creatures from the type of presentation that you would deliver in person. Their purpose is the same—to convey information in a concise way that makes a real impact—but they raise many other issues that need to be thought about carefully.

There are many reasons why people choose, or must, present virtually or online. You may want to add something to your company's website that new customers can visit to find out exactly what you do, for example. Or you may want to showcase an idea or a service to a partner based overseas; you may not be able to justify a business trip to see them, or perhaps the time difference doesn't allow for 'real-time' presentations via the Web.

Whatever the reason, the crucial point is that you yourself will not be there, and so your presentation will need to compensate for this in a number of ways. It must reinforce the image, brand, and overall message of your company; it must engage the audience's attention; it must answer as many of their potential questions as possible, and it must be easy to use.

You'll need to consider how your presentation looks and 'feels', how you can involve the people reading it, and what technology or software you use to create it. The guidelines below will help set you on the right path.

Step one: Think about the length and formatting of your text

As with a face-to-face presentation, the first and most important things to decide are who your audience will be, exactly what you want to say to them, and how to split this into sections to present as slides.

However, there is one big difference: because you won't be there to explain the slides, visuals, or screens, each will have to contain all the explanation necessary. In other words, instead of simply being the written back up to your speech, this presentation must stand alone.

As a result, it will be very tempting to write yards and yards of text to explain everything properly. Don't go there!

TOP TIP
Web page designers work on the premise that reading speeds are more than 25 per cent slower from computer screens than from

**paper. But that doesn't mean you should
write 25 per cent less—you should
write *50* per cent less.**

How you *structure* your text is also important, as people
rarely read screen pages word by word; instead they
scan the page, picking out individual words and sentences.
To cater for this, your copy needs to be very clear and
easily readable in order to get the message across
quickly.

Here's a list of pointers:

✔ keep your sentences short and punchy

✔ make sure that each line is no more than about
12–13 words long

✔ highlight important keywords so that they catch the
reader's eye

✔ use one idea per paragraph, and keep paragraphs
short—no more than three to four lines each

✔ break up the text wherever appropriate with sub-heads,
bullet points, and numbering

✔ make sure your spelling and grammar is top-notch.
Many people adopt a friendlier or more casual tone in

virtual communications than might apply to other
business materials, but spelling mistakes and
grammatical howlers are a step too far.

TOP TIP

To get the *amount* of copy roughly right, write
out your presentation text as if you were
going to deliver it to an audience in person.
Then cut it in half. Then cut it in half
again. That way you will be left with
the important essence of what you
want to say, and none of the extra 'fluff'.

Step two: Get the look and feel right

As with other kinds of presentation, it is important that
the look and feel of an online or virtual presentation are
consistent with the rest of your company image, so that
your audience receives the same key messages from it
as they would from any other contact with your business
(see Chapter 6 for more information on this). In fact, it's
even more important in this case as, once again, you
won't be there in person to reinforce the impression it
creates.

In addition to this, there are other considerations when
designing the look of a virtual or online presentation.
Because reading on screen is much harder on the eyes
than reading on paper, you need to:

✔ avoid cramped text and use as much white space as possible

✔ use a light background with dark text

✔ be careful in your choice of colours. Although these should complement your corporate colours and logo, bright tints like reds and yellows can be dazzling on a screen and difficult to read; paler shades or dark colours are easier on the eyes

✔ choose a simple, non-serif font (like Arial) and a standard font size of 10–12 point

✔ illustrate and enhance key points with tables or simple graphics

✔ aim to keep each page to one screen in length, as most people prefer not to have to scroll too much

---

TOP TIP

Inconsistency or poor quality design will detract from your image, and may even lose you business. Attention to detail, on the other hand, will automatically ensure you come across as professional and even compensate for small shortcomings in content.

Step three: Think about adding some 'drama'

A big advantage of online and virtual presentations is that you can use all sorts of effects to make your information more dramatic and interesting, and thereby catch your audience's attention.

While the important rule here is not to over do it—less really is more!—here are some ideas:

Effect	Description
Orchestrating of information	Use of a pointer to guide the viewer: this could be an ordinary screen pointer, or an animated character of some kind. Try not be too cutesy with this type of thing, though—it might be a good idea to use a character if it ties in with your company logo, for example, but don't go overboard with cuddly toys.
Reveals	This technique allows one piece of information at a time to be presented to the audience, frequently by using a 'grey-out' facility that hides content and reveals it in gradual stages.
Build-ups	Similar to the reveal, this technique allows information to be added in stages.

Overlays	This usually involves the complete image being presented but each 'overlay' highlighting or expanding on the initial image. It can be used to highlight paths through complicated diagrams.
Variety	While all your slides should have a uniting look and feel, it could become boring for the viewer if every screen looks identical. Make sure that there's some variety between them, such as colour coding different subjects.

Step four: Be user-friendly

When you're creating your presentation, it's important to keep the needs of your audience in mind. They are probably busy people with limited time, so you need to make it as easy as possible for them to access the information you're providing.

✔ Explain clearly what your presentation is about on the front page. There's nothing more annoying for people—or anything more likely to lose attention— than having to hunt around to find out what you are talking about. Think perhaps about beginning with a summary of the information you are presenting, with links that click directly through to the different sections so viewers can go straight to areas of interest.

✔ As with a good website, your presentation should be easy to navigate. Try to give readers more than one way to access the information—for example, by having navigation buttons down one side as well as links at the bottom of each page, and cross-reference hyperlinks within the text. If there's a lot of material to get through in your presentation, you might even want to include a simple search facility.

✔ If your presentation requires a lot of detailed information—such as technical specifications, for instance—think about putting it in separate appendices rather than in the main body of the text. That way anyone who needs the in-depth information can find it, while at the same time your main pages remain uncluttered.

✔ Make it easy for readers to contact you should they have questions or require further information. Make sure your phone number or e-mail address can be read clearly and is prominent.

TOP TIP

Give your presentation a human feel, perhaps by including information about, or a photograph of, yourself. This will make your audience feel they are receiving information from an individual, rather than just wading through another piece of anonymous material.

Step five: Think about common queries in advance

✔ Try to anticipate likely questions that people might have after reading your material. Providing the answers in a separate section of your presentation—perhaps in the form of frequently asked questions—will show you're ready to help and may encourage them to contact you. And it may also save you time and money by nipping some basic queries in the bud, such as requests for your opening hours, or prices of the products you're promoting.

Providing an e-mail facility for queries and audience feedback can be useful, but if you do this you must make sure you check your messages regularly and respond promptly or you'll undo all your good work and undermine your professional image.

Step six: Involve your audience

One disadvantage of not presenting your information in person is that it is much harder to make your audience feel involved. However, there are various techniques you can use to hold their attention.

■ **interactivity.** Interactivity is one of the greatest strengths of online technology, and it's a good idea to make your presentation as active as possible. Consider if you can offer online tools such as calculators or quizzes viewers can fill in. These help them feel involved and—if they're useful—will also encourage them to return to your presentation.

■ **changing content.** If your presentation is featured on your website somewhere, you can extend its shelf-life considerably by adding visibly new content on a regular basis. Perhaps you could offer a new tip each day or provide a weekly news service to give visitors a reason to return. This is what is known as 'sticky content'. Remember, to do this you will need to be able to access the presentation to make changes; it will also take a certain amount of time and effort on your part.

■ **freebies.** People are more likely to remember your presentation, and return to it, if they got something useful or free out of their last visit. Is there something you can include that will add value—such as a set of document templates, or a printable poster they could put up on the wall? Perhaps you could even consider providing an incentive such as free entry to a prize draw for giving you feedback?

TOP TIP
It is *essential* that your material is up to date—
readers will be put off immediately if there's
something obviously obsolete on your
presentation, such as an old date at the foot
of it. If the material needs to last some time,
consider removing anything

**time-sensitive from it and keeping dates
as vague as possible, perhaps restricting
them simply to the year of publication.**

Common mistakes

✗ You get carried away

There are so many exciting tools, effects, gadgets, and gizmos that can be used in electronic documents, it can be very easy to overdo it and make your presentation far too busy. Always remember that less is often more and that the main point of your presentation is the information you are trying to convey, not your artistic skills or technical wizardry.

✗ You don't make your presentation easy to access

One vital thing that's easy to forget is how your audience is going to access this presentation of yours. Are you going to e-mail it out, or will you put it on CD and post it? Or do you plan to put it up on the Internet? If it's too complicated or cumbersome, or involves technology that readers don't possess, you will lose them straight away.

As ever, the answer lies mainly in knowing your audience, but generally speaking it's best to keep things as simple as possible. Word documents, for example, are accessible to most PC users, and the files tend to be a manageable size for sending electronically. Powerpoint presentations can be enormous, and very trying to download for anyone who doesn't have a broadband connection. On the other hand, PDF documents require people to have Adobe Acrobat in order to read them: are you sure your readers possess the right software, or can you send out a copy with the presentation? If you want to use the Internet, do you have the right skills to make your presentation look effective and work properly?

If in any doubt, get expert advice—either from your IT department, or from someone experienced in such matters. It would be a pity to fall at the last fence and waste all your hard work!

STEPS TO SUCCESS

✓ Keep your text short, snappy, and punchy.

✓ Check that the look and feel matches the rest of your corporate image, and that it works when displayed on screen.

✓ Add some drama—though judge it carefully.

✓ Be sure that your presentation is user friendly and easy to navigate.

✓ Try to anticipate and answer likely queries arising from your material.

✔ Use clever techniques to involve your audience.

✔ Don't get too carried away with snazzy or unnecessary details and effects.

✔ Make sure that your presentation is not too complicated or high-tech to be easily accessible.

Useful links

Businesslink:
www.businesslink.gov.uk
e-Learning Centre:
www.e-learningcentre.co.uk
University of Strathclyde:
www.strath.ac.uk/Departments/CAP/slides/
frameset5.html
Web Style Guide:
www.webstyleguide.com

Using slides and visuals in your presentation

It's a very common mistake—particularly for those who are new to presenting—to feel that it's necessary to produce a huge number of slides or overheads, containing all the information being discussed, as well as all sorts of complicated and sophisticated diagrams and visuals. You'll be relieved to know that, thankfully, this isn't the case!

In fact, the golden rule is: all written or visual material is only there to back up and give emphasis to what the presenter is saying. That's it. If the audience requires reference material or detailed information, it is far better to produce this as hand outs and give them to people at the end of the presentation, to be taken away and mulled over at leisure. Otherwise, the watchwords are simplicity and clarity.

This chapter provides a series of rules and suggestions which, if followed, will help you to create a presentation that has all the impact necessary, but which may also save you considerable time and effort.

Step one: Think about 'brand consistency'

Whether you're creating slides, visuals, or any other kind of presentation material, it's important to make sure that your audience receives the same key messages from it as they would from any other contact with your business. In other words, the presentation needs to portray the same brand as your website, stationery, sales and marketing materials, offices, signage, or any other promotional literature you might have. If it is not consistent, it may well have a negative impact on how your audience perceives your image in general, so it's worth spending the time to get it right.

Think about the following factors when designing the overall look of your presentation:

- a specific typeface
- your logo and letterhead design
- a particular colour or palette of colours
- any text that needs to be included on every slide— perhaps your website address or business slogan, for example

---

TOP TIP
Even if you're not representing a company or organisation, you still need to create a consistent, professional 'brand' for your presentation. Choosing or designing a

---

**particular template as the basis for each slide
or overhead is a great place to start and will
save you time in the long run.**

**If you're using PowerPoint, use the 'Slide
Master' page to design your overall look
right at the start. By setting up your fonts,
sizes, and colour scheme here, and
inserting any logo you want, they'll
appear on every slide and you won't
have to format each one individually.**

Step two: Create text slides

When creating text slides, there are five main rules to bear in
mind. Get these right and you're well on the way to having an
effective presentation.

1 Make it BIG

You need to choose a font size that's big enough for
everyone to read—even from the back row. As a rough rule
of thumb:

✔ for text in bullet points use a font that's at least 24 pt
in size

✔ for any added detail, use text of at least 18 pt

2 Keep it simple

Most people tend to put too many words on a slide, and it's important to get rid of all unnecessary text. You don't want your audience's attention to be fixed on trying to read a long slide rather than listening to you. The guidelines are:

✔ no more than six lines of text per slide

✔ no more than seven words per line of text

✔ use colour to attract attention to important points—for example, keywords could be highlighted in a different shade.

3 Make it clear

Choose a clear, non-serif font (like Arial) and write in upper and lower case—text that's all in capitals is difficult to read. You also need colours that enhance the readability of your slides. Most of PowerPoint's default font sizes and colour schemes work well; if you decide to experiment with your own, be sure that you don't reduce readability in the process.

TOP TIP

If in doubt, for *printed slides*, dark colours on a light background tend to be the easiest to read; for *projected slides*, light colours on a dark background work best.

---

4 Follow a logical sequence

In order to clarify your message for your audience, the stages of your presentation and the slides you use need to follow a logical sequence. Here are a couple of useful ideas:

✔ Begin and end the presentation with an identical pair of slides, which summarise your main points. At the beginning, this gives the audience a notion of what to expect and helps you conquer last-minute nerves by reminding you of what you want to say. At the end, it provides a way to recap your arguments and also gives the audience the sense that you've come full circle, completing the 'story' you promised them at the beginning.

✔ Create 'signpost' slides, or slides that that remind the audience at intervals where you've got to in the presentation, and how each part fits into the whole. This is a very good way of keeping people's attention— particularly if the presentation is a long one.

TOP TIP
Your audience must be able to get the point of a slide within *five seconds* of seeing it. When you put up a new slide, don't say anything for a few moments—let people absorb the information. Then, when you have their undivided attention, expand upon what the slide has to say.

Step three: Decide on the right visuals

A picture is worth a thousand words, they say—and it's certainly true that a verbal message which is reinforced with a visual one is stronger than the verbal message alone. So visual aids, which in this case means any sort of illustration, graphic, graph, or diagram that you might want to use, are certainly an important part of most presentations.

However, there's a problem: while a good visual gives a huge boost to a presentation, a poor one leaves it worse off than no visual at all. At best, it distracts the audience; at worst, it baffles them. So if you're going to use visuals, it's essential that you use them well.

Your first question, then, when planning your presentation shouldn't be 'what visuals do I need?', but 'do I need any visuals at all?'. Here are three benchmarks to help you decide whether a visual is necessary or not:

1. **Does it back up your argument?** Any visual that doesn't reinforce what you're saying will simply distract the audience.

2. **Does it clarify a tricky point?** Using a picture is sometimes the only effective way to explain something complicated, for example how a machine works, or how different statistics compare with one another.

3. **Does it make an impact?** If there is just one important message you want your audience to take

away from your presentation, can it be summed up in
a single image?

A good example:

One presenter was talking to an audience about 'good
corporate governance' in their organisation—in other
words, getting the whole company into the right mindset
to comply with a series of government regulations. There
could hardly be a drier subject!

But instead of using a series of organisation charts,
workflow diagrams, or illustrations of departmental
responsibilities, the presenter used just one visual: a
picture of the company chief executive, with a set of
prison bars superimposed over his face.

This certainly got the message across: non-compliance
with the regulations could result in big trouble. You
could have heard a pin drop.

Step four: Design visuals

1 Use pictures, not words

The best question to ask yourself when designing a visual is,
'what does this *show*?' (rather than 'what does this *say*?'). In
other words, use as little text as possible. If you do need to
add words—labels on graphs, titles on organisation charts,
stages on workflow diagrams, for example—make sure:

- they're still in a decent font size (18 pt minimum, preferably)
- they're horizontal wherever possible, for ease of reading
- even if they *have* to be vertical (along the bottom axis of a graph, for instance), the letters are horizontal.

2 Try some icebreakers

Sometimes it can be helpful to use a visual early on as an icebreaker that will warm up the audience and to get you over the jitters. Presenters often make this a 'funny', which is fine, but you do need to be a bit careful: if you're not a natural joke teller, it can be embarrassing all round if your funny falls flat. Cartoons can also do the job for you, but again, make sure the content and implications of the cartoon suit the rest of the presentation.

3 Titles for visuals

Too often, presenters make the mistake of putting a general label, such as 'Sales in 2004' at the top of a visual. However, it's much better to come up with a very specific label that tells people what you want them to look at in that visual. Instead, if you wrote 'Sales in 2004 reverse previous downward trend', your audience would know instantly why they're being shown this slide. The key message here is: make the title of a visual the same as its message.

4 Choose the right kind of chart

Charts are the ideal way to convey information instantly. However, different charts are appropriate for different kinds of information. Here's a quick checklist:

Purpose	Chart type and description
Showing change over time (e.g. share prices)	**Line charts**. The slope of the line instantly tells viewers the direction of the trend.
Direct comparisons over time (e.g. how manufacturing costs have risen faster than manufacturing costs over three years)	**Vertical bar chart**. The height of the bars shows the comparative costs; and because people naturally associate left-to-right with the movement of time, vertical bars work better than horizontal ones when there's a time element involved.
Direct comparisons at one time (e.g. the building society with the lowest interest rate in March)	**Horizontal bar chart**. The length of the bar gives its ranking; the label on it identifies the item.
Comparing parts of a whole (e.g. the percentage of government budget spent on education)	**Pie chart**. This is the simplest way to show proportions, as long as there aren't too many slices (five maximum is ideal).
Comparison by geographic location (e.g. sales by region)	**Map**. Distinguish among regions by using different colours, shadings or symbols.

5 Build up an image

If you have a complicated concept to communicate, it can be very effective to break your image up into stages and introduce them one at a time. PowerPoint is the ideal medium for doing this, but you can do it with acetates and flipcharts too.

Say, for example, you're showing an intricate organisational design. You could start with the top executives, then add the directors who report to them, then the group managers, then the departmental heads, and so on. You could do this in a number of ways:

- **sequentially**—separate diagrams for each part, which you show one at a time
- **build-ups**—where each new layer is added individually, one on top of the next
- **reveals**—where you start with the whole diagram, but most of it is covered up to begin with and sections are exposed gradually.

Remember that you may not need to include every single detail of the new organisation in the diagram; just make sure it contains the bits your audience will be interested in.

Step five: Boost your message!

Once you have your visuals, you need to make the best use of them during the presentation to reinforce what you're saying.

✔ Unless a visual is completely obvious or self-explanatory, you need to discuss it—or at least refer to it. It's amazing how many presenters put up a visual and then don't even mention it!

✔ Make sure you don't block audience's view of the visual; you could even step aside for a moment and let people look at it properly.

✔ Once the visual has made its point, take it down—otherwise it might become a distraction.

TOP TIP

A visual doesn't always have to be a design on a slide or overhead: it can also be a prop—a 3-D object that you pass round, for the audience to examine. If you're enthusing about your company's new design of paper clip, for example, there's nothing like letting people handle a real one for ensuring that they remember it.

Common mistakes

✗ **You over-complicate things**

'Keep it simple' is the implicit message throughout all the guidelines above, but it's worth reiterating here. It's extraordinary how many people forget it. Sometimes this is due, ironically, to lack of time—it can take longer to think through a point and boil it down to its essentials than simply to slap down all the available material. It can also be easy to fall for lovely software and graphics packages that tempt you to create fancy effects and animations. Don't! If you bewilder your audience or distract people from your main message, all your efforts will be wasted.

✗ You forget to check for errors

This is one of the commonest ways to shoot yourself in the foot. Your presentation looks lovely, your arguments are sound, your visuals are punchy and effective, BUT . . . you misspell the chief executive's name, or the first word on the title page. Zap goes your credibility, and you'll have to work very hard to build it back up!

STEPS TO SUCCESS

✔ Make sure everything looks consistent and professional, and fits with your business image or brand.

✔ Use big font sizes that can be read from the back row.

✔ Cut out all but essential text.

✔ Check that all fonts and colours are clear and readable.

✔ Follow a logical sequence throughout your presentation.

✔ Decide whether visuals are really necessary.

✔ If so, make sure they're well designed and appropriate to the rest of your presentation.

✔ Think about using props in addition to your visuals.

✔ Be careful not to get too complicated.

✔ Check for errors!

Useful links

Advisory Group on Computer Graphics:
www.agocg.ac.uk/brief/ppt.htm
Awesome Powerpoint Backgrounds:
www.powerpointbackgrounds.com
Business Link:
www.businesslink.gov.uk
KU Medical Center, on-line tutorial series:
www.kumc.edu
Warwick University e-learning guides:
www2.warwick.ac.uk

Surviving worst-case scenarios

In an ideal world, everything would always go as planned. Sadly the world is anything but ideal and as a result, hardly anything ever does! This can be pretty disconcerting, particularly if you're in a situation where you're 'on show', such as giving a presentation. However there are very few circumstances which are completely irredeemable, unless you panic.

It's well worth spending some time thinking through all the things that could possibly go wrong and (if possible) taking preventive action, or (if not) planning what to do in the event. This chapter lays some ground rules . . .

Step one: Make sure you can handle the technology and equipment you need

Technology is a potential problem for every presenter. Even the best designed presentation will fail if the technology you use to deliver it goes wrong, so it's really important to check everything beforehand.

1 Technology

Unless you're using your own equipment, make sure that your presentation will work on what's provided.

- Have you checked that you can load your presentation onto the computer (does it have a CD drive, for example)?
- Does this machine run the same software version that you use? You may be able to run newer presentations under older versions of PowerPoint, for example, but extra features (such as animations or links to other applications) may not work. Check that they do.
- If you need to link to the Web, can you get Internet access?
- Is the projector a relatively new one? Older projectors may be dim and/or have fewer colours.
- Are there enough power points, of the right kinds and in the right places? Will you need extension cables or extra plug sockets, or do you need to rearrange the room?
- Do the connections between different pieces of equipment—from the computer to the projector, for example—work properly?
- If at all possible, run your presentation through from beginning to end in situ.

2 Other equipment

- Make sure you have spares of everything you could need—back-up disks, spare bulbs, spare batteries, extra hand outs, pens, and so on.

- Check that any lectern or stand is at the right height for you.
- Confirm that people will be able to hear properly from all parts of the room, particularly if you're using sound effects or a microphone.
- Have a spare copy of your notes in your briefcase, stapled together and numbered so they can't get mixed up.
- Familiarise yourself with how to operate all the lights, air conditioning, heating, and so on.
- Make sure you know where all the amenities are—coffee rooms, toilets, reception areas, phones, for example— not just for your own information, but so that you can answer if asked by an audience member.

TOP TIP

Be prepared! If you're presenting on home turf, do a practice run-through the day or a few hours before your presentation, so you can check everything mentioned above. If you're presenting elsewhere, liaise with your contact at the venue to find out as much as you can about what equipment is available and what you'll be expected to bring. Arrive at the venue in plenty of time so that you can practise there too.

Step two: Manage the audience

1 Arrange the seating sensibly

There's nothing worse, when presenting, than facing an audience that is scattered all over the room or, even worse, huddled into the back rows of seats leaving a great gulf between you and them. Even the greatest speaker will have difficulty building energy or creating rapport in such circumstances. There are a couple of ways you can prevent such a situation arising:

- if at all possible, find out how many people are coming and put out just enough seats, plus a couple of extras. Arrange them in an arc facing you.
- if you have no idea of, or control over, the numbers attending, tape off the back row of seats and put a 'Reserved' sign on them. Once the front rows are full, remove the sign and let the last arrivals sit at the back.

2 Think about the staging

There are a few other tips for staging the presentation which will also help things run smoothly and enable you to engage with your audience.

✔ Make sure you're not standing with your back to a window, or you'll appear as a silhouette to your listeners.

✔ Check that you have somewhere—like a table—to put

your papers, notes, handouts, briefcase, and anything else you have with you.

✔ If you need to darken the room, make sure you know where light switches are and how curtains or blinds close.

✔ Try sitting in different parts of the room to check that all members of the audience will be able to see properly.

✔ If possible, make sure there's nothing—like a desk or table—between you and your audience. Psychologically it will act as a barrier, and you will have to work that much harder to create rapport.

TOP TIP
Audiences have a very short attention span—
most adults cannot concentrate for more
than seven to ten minutes. To prevent
people from wriggling, chatting, or
switching off, it's a good idea to
break your presentation into easily
digestible sections and change
the pace or create a diversion
at regular intervals.

Step three: Deal with disruptions

Interruptions can put you off your stride, so take preventative action before your presentation begins:

✔ make sure the room is booked well in advance—you don't want another group of people arriving at the same time expecting to have a meeting there!

✔ arrange for any phones in the room to be diverted for the duration

✔ put a sign on the door to stop people from barging in unintentionally

✔ check that there's no regular interruption planned, such as a fire drill. If there is, plan a break around it, or at least tell the audience what will be happening before hand.

✔ fill the seats from the front, as described in the previous section; this has the added benefit of preventing late arrivals from walking all the way to the front and climbing across other people to find somewhere to sit.

✔ if the presentation is likely to be a long one, make sure you schedule plenty of breaks—preferably on the hour, every hour. This helps to eliminate surreptitious escapes to the toilet, and maintains people's concentration.

A difficult situation

Possibly the most difficult disruption you might encounter is if several people in the audience start a side conversation while you are speaking. If this happens, in the following order:

- ask if anyone has any questions
- ask the talkers if you can do anything to clarify
- if they carry on, move closer to them
- if they still don't stop, lower your voice, or pause in what you're saying and look at them
- if all else fails, call a halt to the presentation and ask the whole group whether a new session should be arranged

TOP TIP

You can never expect to eliminate all kinds of interruption, so the golden rule, if you *are* interrupted, is to acknowledge it rather than trying to carry on regardless. If you pause and laugh while a jet plane thunders overhead, for example, the audience will probably laugh too, and the whole episode will actually work to your advantage by creating a bond between you.

Step four: Survive unexpected time issues

Uncertainty about or problems with the time available can throw a presenter completely. Say, for example, the meeting before yours overruns and cuts your time severely . . . what do you do then? The two scenarios below cover most contingencies.

1 You find you have 20 minutes instead of the hour you planned on

Talking quickly isn't the answer! Decide swiftly what proportion of the 20 minutes each part of your presentation should take. Is there any section that could be omitted altogether? Then keep your eye on your watch as you speak and limit yourself to the key concept in each portion.

2 A vital member of the audience has to leave before you've reached your key points

Say the finance director, who has ultimate say over whether his company buys your products, tells you he has to leave early. This could be disastrous. However, there's an old rule regarding presentations: tell people what you're going to tell them, tell them, and then tell them what you told them. If you follow this rule when creating your presentation in the first place, you won't get caught out this way.

✔ Always mention your main point and major supporting points within the first few minutes of any presentation.

✔ If you're using slides or overheads, always have one that contains the main point and the key points.

If, however, you've made the fatal error of trying to save the best for last, ask the decision maker for a moment to summarise (anyone will give you a moment if you ask nicely). Then state, in one sentence, the single point you want the decision maker to remember and, if you have a chance, the two concepts that best support that point.

TOP TIP
It's always worth considering contingencies
when you're creating a presentation.
What would you leave out if your time
were halved? What would your key
messages be if you had five minutes
to tell someone about them?

Step five: Answer difficult questions

Some presenters dread questions from the audience more than anything else, as it's impossible to know what might come up or whether someone might have a particular agenda attached to the question they ask. However, most tricky questions tend to fall into one of only a few categories, and if you recognise these, it will help you know how to answer.

Type of question	Best response
The concealed objection — e.g. 'How come the price is so high?'	• Don't get defensive. • Ask them to clarify the objection — e.g. 'What makes you feel that the price is too high?' • Put it in perspective — e.g. 'It's only a few pence more expensive than its nearest rival . . . '

Type of question	Best response
	• Give the compensating benefits— '. . . and the quality is much higher, so it's actually better value for money.'
The test question, designed to test your knowledge— e.g. 'What are the research findings on side effects for this new drug?'	• Don't bluff. • Call on an expert colleague if you have one there. • If you don't know, say so—but offer to find out later, make a note, and then keep your promise.
The display question, often intended to demonstrate the questioner's own expertise	• Play along and don't be afraid to acknowledge how clever they are publicly. 'Of course you're right—I didn't mention it, simply because I thought it might be too technical for this occasion.'
The challenge question, which usually means you've trespassed on someone else's area of knowledge	• Back down straight away, concede all territorial rights, and perhaps consult their opinion. 'I'm sorry, I meant the transport policy in the West Midlands, not in the whole of the UK—which of course you know more about than I do. Would you say it's the same across the board?'

Type of question	Best response
The defensive question, which tends to mean something you've proposed is a threat to the questioner—e.g. 'Do you really think it's a good idea to let managers train their own staff?'	• Try to question the questioner. 'Could you explain your concerns further, perhaps?' • Throw the question open to the floor . . . do other people feel managers aren't qualified to train their staff? • If it's not within your remit, refer the questioner to someone who *can* provide answers.
The question you plan to discuss in detail later	• Provide a brief answer, then say that you plan to cover the subject properly later. • Don't ask the questioner to wait until you reach the point at which you originally intended to discuss the subject, or everyone will focus on the unanswered question instead of listening to you. • In a meeting setting or small presentation, don't ask people to keep their questions for the end as this suggests that you're not confident enough to deal with interruptions.

TOP TIP
If nothing else, making sure that you know
your stuff and keep calm will usually be
enough to deal with most questions that you
might face.

Step six: Don't let nerves get to you

Almost everyone, even those with lots of experience, suffers from nerves to some degree when they have to present to a group of people. And nerves can make you prone to accidents and stumbling.

However, the one key to solving almost all of these is understanding what causes as attack of nerves: fear, usually of what could possibly go wrong. This is why you generally feel better once you've got going: your equipment's working OK, the audience hasn't booed you off the stage, you haven't made an idiot of yourself, and so on.

The more you pre-empt your fear, then, by doing your preparation thoroughly and taking preventive measures against things that could go wrong, the less nervous you will feel, and the less you'll be to come a cropper. However, even with all the preparation in the world, things can still sometimes go awry. If they do, don't panic—you can still win through. Here are some of the most common nerve-induced pitfalls, and what to do about them:

1 You lose your train of thought mid-sentence

Smile, say 'excuse me' or 'I'm sorry', and start again. Try not to panic or get flustered: it's not the end of the world and everyone in the room has lost track of an idea at least once in their lives. People want you to succeed and are generally sympathetic. Keep smiling.

2 Your throat dries up

Actors have a good trick for dealing with this. Roll a tiny piece of paper into a small ball and place it between your gum and the inside of your cheek at the back of your mouth. It will stimulate the flow of saliva, just like that little roll of cotton wool the dentist uses. Try this in private first, however, so you are sure you are comfortable.

3 You drop your overheads on the floor

Make a joke about your clumsiness, pick them up and take a few moments to put them in order. (Now is the time to be grateful you have numbered them.)

Common mistakes

✗ You don't rehearse

Almost every piece of advice in this actionlist points to one thing: you MUST PRACTISE! With plenty of rehearsal, your confidence will be sufficient to see you through just about any disaster. It's not enough to say your presentation over to yourself in your head, as it's very different when you have to get up and do it in front of an audience. Choose a friend or colleague who you trust, and ask them if they will watch you and give you honest feedback. As an absolute minimum, stand in front of a mirror and run through the presentation, checking yourself as critically as you can.

STEPS TO SUCCESS

✔ In order to pre-empt disasters with equipment, check thoroughly that everything works, in situ, **before** the presentation starts.

✔ Arrange the seating and staging in the best way to help build rapport with your audience and to maintain their concentration.

✔ Take pre-emptive measures to avoid interruptions.

✔ Have contingency plans in case the time available alters significantly.

✔ Learn to handle difficult questions.

✔ Manage your nerves by addressing the fear behind them.

✔ Practise, practise, practise.

Useful links

Business Link:

www.businesslink.gov.uk

KU Medical Center, on-line tutorial series:

www.kumc.edu

Strategic Communications:

www.strategiccomm.com/disasters.html

Where to find more help

Don't Sweat the Small Stuff
Richard Carlson
London: Hodder Mobius, 1999
284pp ISBN: 0340748737
This is a best-selling comprehensive guide to combating stress in
your life at work. The book is full of useful advice for dealing with a
range of panic-inducing situations, including presentations and
meetings.

**Effective Presentation: How to Create and Deliver
a Winning Presentation**
Antony Jay, Ros Jay
Harlow: Prentice Hall, 1999
174pp (Smarter Solutions series)
ISBN: 027364498X
Drawing on their own experience and on tips from experts and
trainers in presentation and communication skills, the authors offer a
step-by-step guide to planning, designing, and delivering successful
presentations. They give advice on scheduling and staging the
presentation, choosing appropriate visual aids, and engaging the
audience.

**Point, Click and Wow!: A Quick Guide to Brilliant
Laptop Presentations**
2nd ed
Claudyne Wilder, Jennifer Rotondo
Chichester: Jossey-Bass Wiley, 2002
240pp ISBN: 0787956694
Aimed at business people of all levels, this book offers a practical
guide to using technology in effective presentations. The authors
explore how to balance on-screen activity and human interaction,
how to deal with software and hardware issues, and how, when,
and where to practise. The book includes checklists and
illustrations.

Index

adrenalin 29–30
audience:
 attention span 77
 disruptions 77–9
 interacting with 24
 researching 3–4, 12–13
 seating arrangements 76, 78
 time problems 80–1
 virtual or online presentations 48,
  53–4, 55–6
 see also questions

body language 3, 35–46
'brand consistency' 61–2
breaks 11–12, 78
breathing 27–8, 31

CD-ROMs 10
charts 7, 67–9
clothes 43–4
colours, slides 62, 63
communication, non-verbal
 35–46
conclusion 18–19
confidence 32–3
contingency plans 9–10, 81
cue cards 10–11

delivery 19–20
designing visual aids 66–9
disruptions 77–9
'drama', virtual or online presentations
 52–3

e-mails 10, 55
enthusiasm 22–3
entrances 36
equipment 8, 23
 rehearsals 9, 12
 worst-case scenarios 73–5
exits 22

expressions, facial 20, 35, 43
eye contact 19, 40, 45

facial expressions 20, 35, 43
fear 29–30
'fight or flight' response 29–30
font sizes, text slides 62, 63

gestures 19, 38–9, 45

handouts 7, 9, 22, 60

icebreakers, visual aids 67
information:
 researching facts 4–5
 visual aids 8, 9, 60–72
interruptions 77–9
introductions 16–17

jargon 7
jokes 67

Kinnock, Neil 38

language, jargon 7

mannerisms 38–9, 41–2
mental preparation 30–1
microphones 11, 75

nervousness 26–34, 36–7, 84–5
non-verbal communication 35–46

online presentations 47–59
overheads see visual aids

pictures, visual aids 65–7
positive thinking 27
posture 19–20, 35, 36–7, 45
PowerPoint 8, 58, 62, 69, 74
practising 8–11, 75, 85–6
presentations:
 body language 3, 35–46
 length 13
 nervousness 26–34, 36–7, 84–5

objectives 2
posture and delivery 19–20
practising 8–11, 33, 75, 85–6
question-and-answer sessions 10,
 21, 30–1
structure of 15–19
venues 11–12, 13
virtual or online 47–59
visual aids 8, 9, 12, 23, 60–72
worst-case scenarios 73–87
writing speeches 6–7
props 39, 70

questions:
 difficult questions 81–4
 preparing for 30–1
 question-and-answer sessions 10,
  21
 virtual or online presentations 55

receptionists 12
refreshments 11–12
rehearsals 8–11, 33, 75, 85–6
relaxation techniques 31–2
research 3–5, 12–13

seating arrangements 76, 78
shyness 28–9
slides 60–4
software 57–8, 74
speeches:
 clarity 20, 23, 42
 length of 10
 practising 8–11, 33
 writing 6–7
staging 76–7

structure 15–19
 virtual or online presentations 49–50
 visual aid sequences 64

technology see equipment
text slides 62–4
throat, drying up 85
time problems 79–81
timing 40–1
titles, visual aids 67
tone of voice 35, 41–2
train of thought, losing 85
travel 24

venues 11–12, 13
virtual presentations 47–59
visual aids 8, 60–72
 'brand consistency' 61–2
 designing 66–9
 dropping overheads 85
 pictures 65–6
 preparation 23
 rehearsals 9
 text slides 62–4
visualisation 30
voice:
 throat drying up 85
 tone of 35, 41–2
 varying 20

websites 47–59
worst-case scenarios 73–87
writing:
 speeches 6–7
 virtual or online presentations
  49–50